Farm Animals

PIGS ON THE FARM

By Rose Carraway

Please visit our website, www.garethstevens.com. For a free color catalog of all our high-quality books, call toll free 1-800-542-2595 or fax 1-877-542-2596.

Library of Congress Cataloging-in-Publication Data

Carraway, Rose.
 Pigs on the farm / Rose Carraway.
     p. cm. — (Farm animals)
 Includes index.
 ISBN 978-1-4339-7361-1 (pbk.)
 ISBN 978-1-4339-7362-8 (6-pack)
 ISBN 978-1-4339-7360-4 (library binding)
 1. Swine—Juvenile literature. I. Title.
 SF395.5.C37 2013
 636.4'0887—dc23
                                    2011051821

First Edition

Published in 2013 by
Gareth Stevens Publishing
111 East 14th Street, Suite 349
New York, NY 10003

Copyright © 2013 Gareth Stevens Publishing

Editor: Katie Kawa
Designer: Andrea Davison-Bartolotta

Photo credits: Cover, p. 1 Ppaauullee/Shutterstock.com; p. 5 © iStockphoto.com/Kay Ransom; pp. 7, 11, 17, 19, 23 (bottom), 24 (straw) iStockphoto/Thinkstock; p. 9 © iStockphoto.com/James Pauls; p. 13 © iStockphoto.com/Craig W. Walsh; p. 15 hvoya/Shutterstock.com; pp. 21, 24 Uwe Pillat/Shutterstock.com; pp. 23 (top), 24 (tail) Tsekhmister/Shutterstock.com.

All rights reserved. No part of this book may be reproduced in any form without permission in writing from the publisher, except by a reviewer.

Printed in the United States of America

CPSIA compliance information: Batch #CS12GS: For further information contact Gareth Stevens, New York, New York at 1-800-542-2595.

Contents

Smart Animals 4

Life on the Farm 14

Teeth and Tails 20

Words to Know 24

Index 24

A farm where pigs live is called a piggery.

Pigs are very smart!
They can learn tricks.

7

A pig can come
when a person calls
its name.

Pigs talk to each other!
They use sounds
called grunts.

A mother pig is a sow.
Baby pigs are piglets.

Pigs roll in the mud to stay cool.

15

A pig sleeps
on top of straw.

Pigs eat corn.
A farmer feeds them every day.

A pig has 44 teeth!

Some pigs have straight tails. Some have curly tails.

Words to Know

straw tail teeth

Index

piggery 4   sow 12
piglets 12   teeth 20